What Are Rules at School?

by Margaret McNamara

Table of Contents

Words to Think About 2
Introduction 4
Chapter 1 Rules Help You Learn 6
Chapter 2 Rules Keep You Safe 8
Chapter 3 Rules Teach Respect 10
Chapter 4 Rules Help You Take Care of Your School 12
Conclusion 14
Glossary and Index 16

Words to Think About

citizens

These students are good citizens.

community

People work and play together in our school community.

respect

We show respect for others by reading quietly.

rules

This poster shows us the rules, or things we need to do.

safe

Walking, instead of running, keeps us safe.

school

School is a place to learn.

Introduction

All good **citizens**, or members of a **community**, follow **rules**. Rules tell people what they should and shouldn't do.

Your **school** is a community. Your school has rules. In this book, you'll learn about rules at school.

▲ People need to follow rules in school.

Chapter 1

Rules Help You Learn

Students learn best when they get to school on time and pay attention. They also need to do their homework.

▲ This student follows a rule about doing homework.

Teachers make rules so you will do these things. They want you to do your best in school.

> **Rules at Your School**
>
> What rules help you learn?

Rules Keep You Safe

If you run down the halls, then you can fall or bump into others. If you do a science experiment without wearing safety equipment, you can get hurt.

Schools make rules so that you don't get hurt. The rules tell you how to be **safe**.

Rules at Your School

What rules keep you safe?

▲ Goggles keep your eyes safe during an experiment.

Rules Teach Respect

Good citizens treat others with **respect**. If you tease other students, then you are not showing respect. You show respect when you wait your turn to speak.

Schools want you to be a good citizen. They make rules to teach you respect.

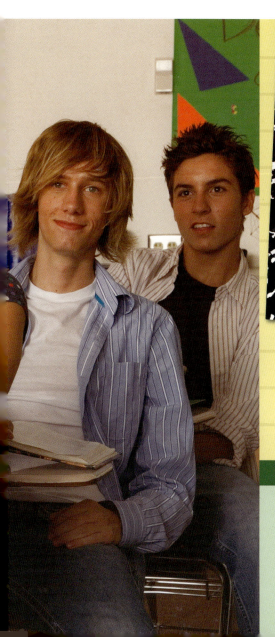

▲ Which rules help students show respect?

LOOK AT TEXT STRUCTURE

Cause and Effect

The word "if" shows a cause. The cause is teasing other students. The word "then" shows the effect.

Chapter 4

Rules Help You Take Care of Your School

Many people work, learn, and play at your school. Everyone needs to take care of the school, too.

Some rules tell you how to keep the school clean. Some rules tell you how you can make the school better.

Rules at Your School

What rules help you take care of your school?

Conclusion

Your school is a community. When you follow rules at school, you are a good citizen.

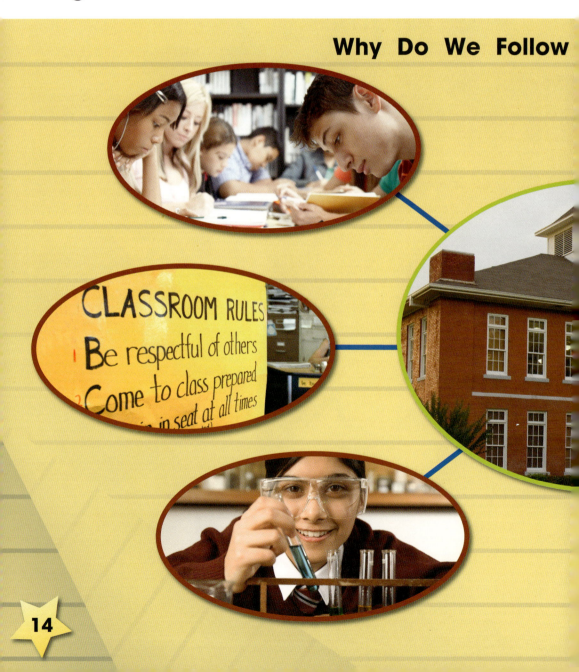

Why Do We Follow

Rules at school help you learn, stay safe, and respect others. Rules help you take care of the school, too.

Rules at School?

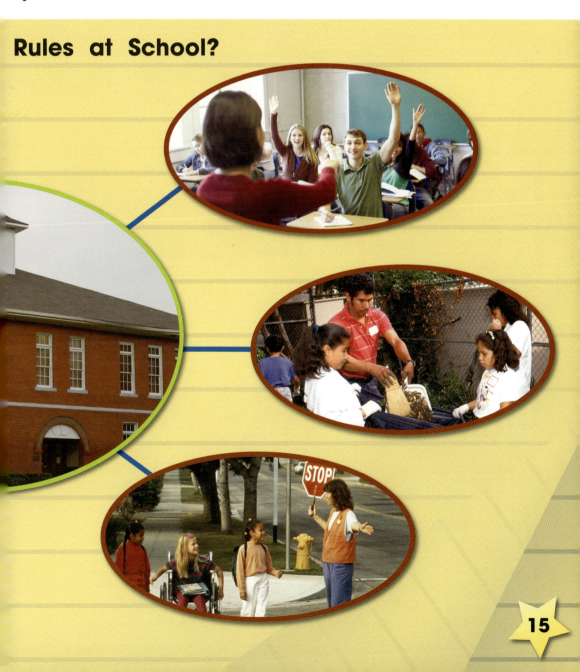

Glossary

citizens the people who are part of a community

See page 4.

community a place where people work and play together

See page 4.

respect care and concern for others

See page 10.

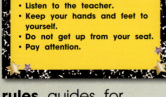

rules guides for what must happen

See page 4.

safe not getting hurt

See page 9.

school a place that people go to learn

See page 5.

Index

citizens, 4, 10–11, 14

community, 4–5, 14

respect, 10–11, 15

rules, 4–5, 7, 9, 11, 13–15

safe, 9, 15

school, 5–7, 9, 11–15

Career CONNECTION

Principal

A principal is the person who is in charge of a school.

Sometimes the principal can help students solve problems.

The principal has an important job. This person keeps the school running smoothly.

Principals make sure teachers are teaching what students need to learn.

Many principals were teachers before they became principals.

Make a Connection

What would be the best thing about being the principal of your school? Why?

Content CONNECTIONS™

What Are Some Rules at School?

Why do schools have rules? Why is it important to follow rules? Read about some rules at school and how following rules can help you.

Theme: Rules and Government

ABOUT THE AUTHOR
Margaret McNamara was a teacher for many years. Now she writes books for students. Margaret lives near a lake. She enjoys reading, canoeing, and bicycling.

BENCHMARK EDUCATION COMPANY

ISBN 978-1-60634-526-9

GENRE readers' & writers' WORKSHOP

INFORMATIONAL TEXTS

Science at Sea

by Jeanette Leardi

GENRE: Informational Texts

GENRE readers' & writers' WORKSHOP™

Level* U/50
Lexile® 790L

LITERARY ANALYSIS
- Respond to and interpret text
- Make text-to-text connections
- Analyze the genre

READING SKILLS
Comprehension
- Make judgments
- Draw conclusions

Word Study
- Word origins

Tier Two Vocabulary
(see Glossary)

WRITING SKILLS
Writer's Tools
- Strong ending

Writer's Craft
- How to write an informational text

THEME CONNECTIONS
- Science and Technology

*The reading level assigned to this text is based on the genre examples only. "Focus on the Genre," "Reread," and "Writer's Craft" features were not leveled. These sections are intended for read-aloud or shared reading.

Benchmark Education Company
145 Huguenot Street
New Rochelle, NY • 10801

© Benchmark Education Company, LLC. All rights reserved. No part of this publication may be reproduced or transmitted in any form or by any means, electronic or mechanical, including photocopy, recording, or any information storage and retrieval system, without permission in writing from the publisher.

LEXILE® is a trademark of MetaMetrics, Inc., and is registered in the United States and abroad.

Printed in Guangzhou, China.
4401/1219/CA21902064

ISBN: 978-1-4509-5323-8

How to use this book

1. Learn about informational texts by reading pages 2–3. Get background information about the articles on page 5. (Shared reading)

2. Read the articles for enjoyment. (Leveled texts)

3. Reread the articles and answer the questions on pages 14–15, 21, and 28–29. (Shared reading)

4. Reread the last article. Pay attention to the comments in the margins. See how an author writes an informational text. (Leveled text)

5. Follow the steps on pages 30–31 to write your own informational text. (Shared reading)

6. Complete the activity on the inside back cover. Answer the follow-up questions. (Shared reading)

Credits
Project Editor: Jeffrey B. Fuerst
Creative Director: Laurie Berger
Senior Art Director: Glenn Davis
Director of Photography: Doug Schneider
Photo Editor: Diane French
English Language Arts Advisor: Donna Schmeltekopf Clark

Photo credits: Cover: ©Norbert Wu/Science Faction/Corbis; Page 9A: Courtesy Dr. Laurence Padman Earth & Space Research Corvallis, OR; Page 10A: ©Ralph White/Corbis; Page 10B: AP Image; Page 11A: ©Bettmann/Corbis; Page 11B: Romeo Gacad/AFP/Getty Images/Newscom; Page 12: Steve Mcalister; Page 13B: National Geographic/Getty Images; Page 17A: Dr. D. P. Wilson/Photo Researchers, Inc.; Page 17B: Peter Scoones/Photo Researchers, Inc.; Page 20C: ©Jonathan Blair/Corbis; Page 20D: Roger Munns, Scubazoo/Photo Researchers, Inc.; Page 22: Ambient Images/Photolibrary; Page 25: Jan Halaska/Photo Researchers, Inc.; Page 26: ANT Photo Library/Photo Researchers, Inc.; Page 27: Michael Patrick O'Neill/Photo Researchers, Inc.; Page 28: Pierre Huguet/Photolibrary

Toll-Free 1-877-236-2465
www.benchmarkeducation.com
www.benchmarkuniverse.com